P9-BJS-388

Acquaintance I would have, but when't depends
Not on the number, but the choice of friends.

Abraham Cowley
"Of Myself"

IN PRAISE OF

FRIENDSHIP

SMITHMARK

Copyright © The Image Bank 1992. All rights reserved.

This edition published in 1992 by SMITHMARK
Publishers Inc., 112 Madison Avenue, New York, N.Y. 10016
ISBN 0-8317-5009-X
Printed and bound in Hong Kong
Producer: Solomon M. Skolnick *Designer:* Ann-Louise Lipman
Editor: Sara Colacurto *Production:* Valerie Zars
Photo Researcher: Edward Douglas *Assistant Photo
Researcher:* Robert V. Hale *Editorial Assistant:*
Carol Raguso

Index of Photographers

All photographs courtesy of The Image Bank. For information contact
The Image Bank, 111 Fifth Avenue, New York, N.Y. 10003

Shoji Yoshida endpaper. **David Brownell** 4. **Yuri Dojc** 5. **Dann Coffey** 7. **Elyse Lewin** 8-9,
21, 25. **Stephen Marks/Stockphotos, Inc.** 10. **Grant V. Faint** 11, 28. **Walter Bibikow**
12-13. **André Gallant** 15. **Janeart Ltd.** 16. **Margaret W. Peterson** 17. **Kenneth Redding**
19. **Grafton Smith** 20. **Mel DiGiacomo** 23. **Zoa-Longfield** 24. **G & M David De Lossy** 26.
David W. Hamilton 27.

Forsake not an old friend; for
a new one is not comparable
to him: a new friend is as new
wine; when it is old, thou shalt
drink it with pleasure.

Ecclesiasticus 9:10

For memory has painted this perfect day
With colors that never fade,
And we find at the end of a perfect day
The soul of a friend we've made.

Carrie Jacobs Bond
"A Perfect Day"

True friendship is like sound
health; the value of it is seldom
known until it be lost.

Charles Caleb Colton
Lacon

Don't put your friend in your pocket.

Irish Proverb

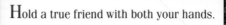

Hold a true friend with both your hands.

Nigerian Proverb

I keep my friends as misers do their
treasure, because, of all the things
granted us by wisdom, none is greater
or better than friendship.

Pietro Aretino
Letter to Giovanni Pollastra
July 7, 1537

Friendship is a strong and habitual inclination in two persons to promote the good and happiness of one another.

Eustace Budgell
in *The Spectator*

The most I can do for my friend is
simply to be his friend.

Henry David Thoreau
Journal
February 7, 1841

A companion loves some agreeable
qualities which a man may possess,
but a friend loves the man himself.

James Boswell
London Journal
July 7, 1763

It is one of the blessings of old friends
that you can afford to be stupid
with them.

Ralph Waldo Emerson
Journals
1836

That friendship may be at once fond and lasting, there must not only be equal virtue on each part, but virtue of the same kind; not only the same end must be proposed, but the same means must be approved by both.

Samuel Johnson
The Rambler

A Father's a Treasure; a
Brother's a Comfort; a Friend
is both.

Benjamin Franklin
Poor Richard's Almanac

A man cannot be said to succeed in this life who does not satisfy one friend.

Henry David Thoreau
Journal
February 19, 1857

The happiest moments it [my heart] knows are those in which it is pouring forth its affections to a few esteemed characters.

Thomas Jefferson
Letter to Eliza House Trist
December 15, 1786

Fame is the scentless sunflower, with gaudy
        crown of gold;
But friendship is the breathing rose, with
        sweets in every fold.

Oliver Wendell Holmes, Sr.
"No Time Like the Old Time"

A friend's only gift is himself. . . . To praise the
utility of friendship, as the ancients so often did,
and to regard it as a political institution justified,
like victory or government, by its material results,
is to lose one's moral bearings. . . . We are not to
look now for what makes friendship useful, but for
whatever may be found in friendship that may
lend utility to life.

George Santayana
The Life of Reason

"Friendship is Love without his wings!"

George Noel Gordon, Lord Byron
L'Amitié Est l'Amour sans Ailes

You cannot be friends upon any other terms than upon the terms of equality.

Woodrow Wilson
Speech, October 27, 1913

A faithful friend is a strong defense: and he that hath found such an one hath found a treasure.

Ecclesiasticus 6:14

A friend may well be reckoned the
masterpiece of Nature.

Ralph Waldo Emerson
''Friendship''
Essays: First Series

Happy is the house that shelters a friend.

Ralph Waldo Emerson
"Friendship"
Essays: First Series

From quiet homes and first beginning,
Out to the undiscovered ends,
There's nothing worth the wear of winning,
But laughter and the love of friends.

Hilaire Belloc
"Dedicatory Ode"
Verses

And the song, from beginning to end,
I found in the heart of an old friend.

Henry Wadsworth Longfellow
"The Arrow and the Song"

Yes'm, old friends is always best,
'less you can catch a new one that's
fit to make an old one out of.

Sarah Orne Jewett
The Country of the Pointed Firs

If a man does not make new acquaintances as he advances through life, he will soon find himself left alone. A man, sir, should keep his friendship in a constant repair.

Samuel Johnson
Letter to Lord Chesterfield
February 7, 1754